in the heart of Hope

All images © Hulton Getty Picture Collection
Design by Keith Jackson
Picture research by Jon Wright
All text, unless otherwise attributed, by Jonathan Bicknell.

Developed by Publishing Services Corp., Nashville, Tennessee.

Published by C. R. Gibson®
C. R. Gibson® is a registered trademark of Thomas Nelson, Inc.
Nashville, Tennessee 37214
Printed and bound by L. Rex Printing Company Limited, China

ISBN 0-7667-7597-6
UPC 0-82272-47485-7
GB 103

in the heart of Hope

"For when hope does awaken, an entire life awakens along with it."

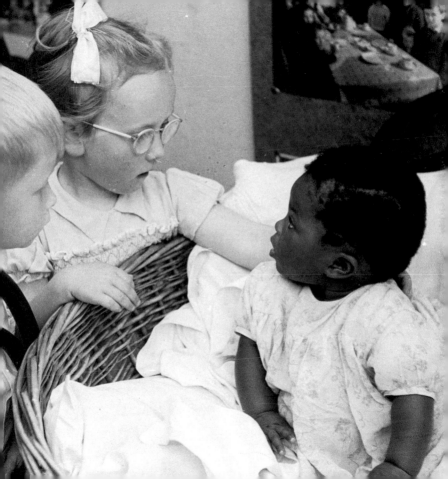

"Hope hangs in there!"

"All things are possible to the one who believes. Yet more to the one who hopes."

Brother Lawrence

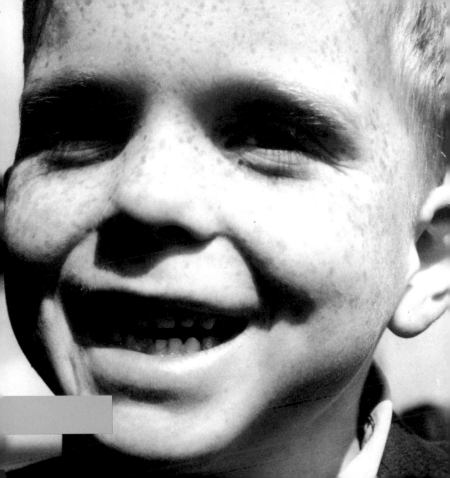

"If you do not hope, you will not find what is beyond your hopes."

Clement of Alexandria

"Don't be afraid of greatness. Some are born great..."

"...some achieve greatness..."

"...and some have greatness thrust upon them."

William Shakespeare

"Dream the impossible dream. Dreaming it may make it possible. It often has."

"And one day soon your day will come. So just keep at it!"

"Pessimists invest in nothing, but optimists invest in hope."

"Hope understands that the darkest hour is the one just before the dawn."

"But I can't do it alone. With you I can face the future."

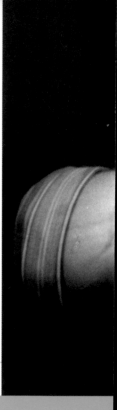

"The crowd, the world, and sometimes the grave step aside for the ones who know where they are going."

Latin Proverb

"Life has its own sweet surprises."

"Hope springs eternal."